Pump it up
Magazine
AF351322
Vol.8
Issue #6
-
June
2023
Grab Your
RollerSkate!
Let's Roll into Summer Wellness
Beauty Secret
Glow Up with Microneedling
Get in Shape With our Fitness Program
Fitness
What's Hot?!
Eating Well For Your Mental Health
Fun Quizz
Indie Music Artist Discovery
Jan Daley
Inspiring Empowerment
Through Music
and an Inductee of
the Women Songwriters Hall of Fame!
Fashion
How to look expensive!
From Narcissistic Abuse to Musical Resilience: A Poignant Journey of Unconditional Love

Union Station - 50 Massachusetts Ave NE
Washington DC, 20002

TICKETS
www.womensongwritershalloffame.org

Pump it up Magazine

TABLE OF CONTENTS

Pump it up MAGAZINE ®

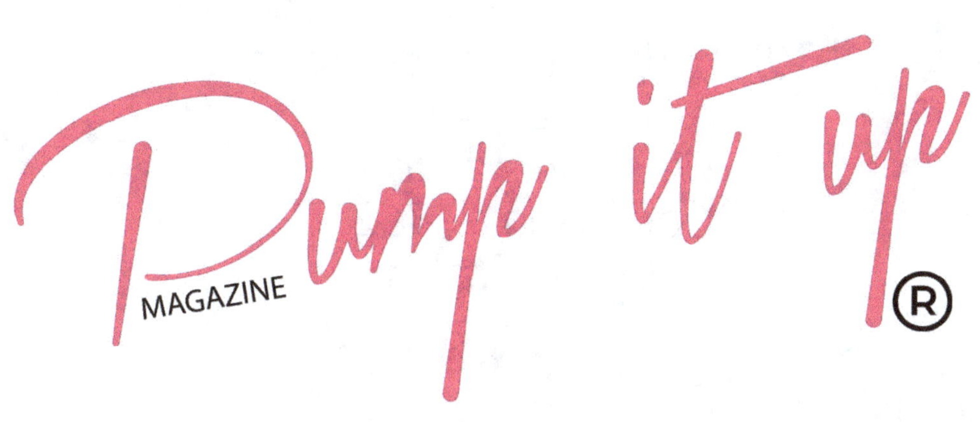

PUMP IT UP MAGAZINE ───────

LINKS

WEBSITE
www.pumpitupmagazine.com

FACEBOOK
www.facebook.com/pumpitupmagazine

TWITTER
www.twitter.com/pumpitupmag

SOUNDCLOUD
www.soundcloud.com/pumpitupmagazine

INSTAGRAM
pumpitupmagazine

PINTEREST
www.pinterest.com/pumpitupmagazine

PUMP IT UP MAGAZINE
30721 Russell Ranch Road
Suite 140
Westlake Village,
California 91362
United States

 (818)514 – 0038(Ext:102)
 info@pumpitupmagazine.com

Welcome to the June 2023 edition of Pump it up Magazine! This month, we proudly feature Jan Daley, celebrating her induction into the Women Songwriters Hall of Fame with her powerful single, 'The Way of a Woman.' Join us as we explore the captivating world of artistry, wellness, and resilience.

Get ready to embrace the thrill of roller skating! Whether you're experienced or a beginner, we've got you covered with tips, tricks, and recommendations to make your roller skating experience memorable.

Unlock the secrets to a radiant glow with microneedling. Delve into its science and effectiveness as we share success stories. Discover how microneedling can transform your skin, leaving you with a youthful and vibrant appearance.

Make this summer the season of fitness as we guide you through a comprehensive program. Focus on holistic well-being and achieve your fitness goals.

Explore the connection between nutrition and mental health. Empower yourself with expert advice and practical tips for a healthier mind and body.

Immerse yourself in the world of indie music and discover feel-good artists who enhance your summer experience. Unearth hidden gems and expand your musical horizons as you embrace the feel-good vibes of warmth and sunshine.

Exude elegance and style without breaking the bank. Learn the secrets to achieving an expensive look on any budget.

Witness the inspiring journey of an artist who triumphed over narcissistic abuse, finding solace and resilience through music. Experience the healing power of art and the strength of the human spirit, highlighting the transformative impact of unconditional love.

Immerse yourself in the world of music, wellness, beauty, and fashion within these pages. Jan Daley's talent and indomitable spirit set the tone for an issue filled with inspiration and empowerment.

May this edition of Pump it up Magazine ignite your passion and uplift your spirits.

Happy reading!

Anissa Sutton

CONTRIBUTORS

FOUNDER
Anissa Sutton

EDITOR
Michael B. Sutton

MARKETING
Grace Rose

PARTNERS

Editions L.A.
editions-la.com

The Sound Of L.A.
thesoundofla.com

Info Music
infomusic.fr

YMC
YourMusicConsultant.Com

BBL
bilingualbookstore.com

WEO
westendorganix.com

Jan Daley
Jazz - Smooth Jazz Singer - Songwriter
2023 Women Songwriters Hall of Fame Inductee

Jan Daley Inducted into Women Songwriters Hall of Fame, Releases Emotional Single "The Way of a Woman"

It is with great excitement that we announce Jan Daley's induction into the esteemed Women Songwriters Hall of Fame, honoring her exceptional contributions to the music industry as a talented and accomplished artist. This prestigious recognition coincides with the release of her latest single, "The Way of a Woman," a deeply poignant and introspective composition.

"The Way of a Woman" explores the intricate complexities and struggles faced by women in relationships, shedding light on the profound pain of infidelity. With lyrics that tug at the heartstrings, the song calls upon society to acknowledge the far-reaching impact of cheating and work towards finding meaningful solutions. Infidelity remains an all-too-common issue that can leave individuals and relationships devastated.

Since its release, "The Way of a Woman" has made an indelible impact in the music industry, swiftly ascending to an impressive #25 position on the Mediabase Mainstream charts, rubbing shoulders with the likes of renowned artists such as Lady Gaga, Taylor Swift, and Miley Cyrus. Additionally, the song has secured the coveted #4 spot on the Mediabase Independent Adult Contemporary chart, solidifying its position as a powerful and resonant composition.

Furthermore, Jan Daley's eponymous album, "The Way of a Woman," has enjoyed remarkable success on the charts. The album's exceptional jazz compositions propelled it to an impressive two-week reign at the #1 position on the Billboard Jazz chart, showcasing Jan Daley's versatility and her ability to captivate jazz enthusiasts worldwide.

Jan Daley's induction into the Women Songwriters Hall of Fame solidifies her as a trailblazing artist, inspiring musicians worldwide. Don't miss her special performance of "The Way of a Woman - Women Songwriters Hall of Fame Version" on June 24th in Washington, DC.

Get your tickets now at www.womensongwritershalloffame.org.

In addition, exciting projects are on the horizon for Jan Daley and "The Way of a Woman." Stay tuned for the upcoming release of a smooth jazz version, a dance remixes EP, featuring electrifying versions that will get you on your feet. Furthermore, prepare yourself for the captivating "Dusty Boots Mix," a country rendition that adds a unique twist to the beloved single.

Keep an eye out for these thrilling releases on Jan Daley's official website at www.jandaley.com.

THE WAY OF A WOMAN
JAN DALEY
JUNE 24 SAT 7PM
LIVE PERFORMANCE
WOMEN SONGWRITERS
HALL OF FAME
WWW.JANDALEY.COM

Jan Daley:
A Musical Phenomenon Empowering Audiences Worldwide

Jan Daley is an extraordinary singer, actress, and songwriter who has captivated audiences around the globe with her singular talent and unwavering commitment to her craft. Adored for her ability to make classic music contemporary again, she is hailed as the best-kept secret in entertainment today. With a remarkable career spanning multiple decades, Jan Daley has solidified her position as a true icon in the music industry.

From the moment she takes the stage, Jan Daley's magical presence shines through. She possesses a rare gift of taking the iconic sound of traditional jazz and reimagining it for modern audiences to enjoy. Her performances hit the sweet spot between authentic, personal delivery and a touch of razzle-dazzle, leaving audiences captivated and yearning for more.

Jan Daley's musical versatility is truly unmatched. With her immense talent, she effortlessly navigates various genres, from jazz to Broadway hits and from faith-fueled albums to dance music. Her dedication to delivering exceptional music is evident in her numerous successful albums, each showcasing her unique artistry and vocal prowess.

"The Way of a Woman," Jan Daley's chart-topping album, has mesmerized listeners worldwide. With exceptional jazz compositions that push boundaries and evoke powerful emotions, the album secured the coveted #1 position on the Billboard Jazz chart for an impressive two weeks. Jan Daley's ability to breathe new life into traditional jazz has earned her the admiration of both critics and fans alike.

In recognition of her exceptional talent and contributions, Jan Daley was inducted into the esteemed Women Songwriters Hall of Fame. This prestigious honor serves as a testament to her unwavering dedication and extraordinary songwriting abilities. To celebrate this momentous achievement, Jan Daley will perform "The Way of a Woman - Women Songwriters Hall of Fame Version" on June 24th in Washington, DC. This special performance promises to be a mesmerizing experience that showcases Jan's unparalleled artistry and her undeniable impact on the music industry.

Jan Daley's impact extends far beyond the charts and stages. She has used her music to empower and uplift women, creating a sense of unity and strength through her powerful lyrics. Her single "The Way of a Woman - WSHOF Version" has become an anthem for resilience and female empowerment, resonating deeply with listeners around the world. Through her music, Jan Daley inspires aspiring artists and highlights the significant role women have played in shaping the music industry.

Beyond her musical accomplishments, Jan Daley has graced both the small and big screens, showcasing her remarkable acting talent alongside industry legends. From appearances on popular shows like The Tonight Show and The Merv Griffin Show to starring in movies alongside Bruce Willis and Tom Hanks, Jan's acting career is as impressive as her musical journey.

Jan Daley's incredible journey has touched the hearts of audiences everywhere. Her performances on Access Hollywood and exclusive interviews on ABC 7 News have provided a glimpse into her remarkable life and career. Through captivating stories of triumph and heartfelt tributes to her late father, who tragically lost his life while serving his country, Jan Daley continues to inspire and uplift.

With her chart-topping success, induction into the Women Songwriters Hall of Fame, and her relentless pursuit of excellence, Jan Daley stands as a beacon of talent and inspiration in the entertainment industry. Her ability to connect with audiences on a profound level and her unwavering commitment to her craft have solidified her status as a musical phenomenon.

To experience the magic of Jan Daley's music and learn more about her inspiring journey, visit her official website at www.JanDaley.com. Follow her on social media @JanDaleyMusic to stay updated on her latest projects, performances, and empowering messages. Jan Daley continues to leave an indelible mark on the music industry and the hearts of all who have the pleasure of hearing her extraordinary voice.

Women Songwriters Hall Of Fame Inductee
THE WAY OF A WOMAN
WSHOF Version
Jan Daley
WSHOF

Enjoy The Sound Of

Pump it up

RADIO

Get the free Pump it up magazine Radio App on your smartphone or tablet, and you'll never miss your favourite music !

POP - ROCK - DANCE - RNB - JAZZ
Available on Google Play Store
www.PumpItUpMagazine.com

HOW MUSIC FOR THE ROLLER RINK IMPACTED THE CLUB

Moodymann's Soul Skate party embodies a long tradition where rollerskating and club music intertwine. We spoke with Kenny Dixon Jr., Traci Washington, Louie Vega, Danny Krivit and more on one of America's richest subcultures.

When you show up to Detroit's Northland Roller Rink during Soul Skate, you enter a different world. Thousands of skaters, along with a few hundred Moodymann fans, crowd onto the burnished hardwood floor. Look closely, and you'll observe nuanced regional skate styles honed in cities like Atlanta, Philadelphia and LA throughout the year. Skate scene DJs like DJ Arson play sub-110 BPM grooves to keep things rolling smooth. Detroit locals greet visitors like family. 80-year-olds put you to shame on skates.

Back in 2007, I showed up at Northland for the first Soul Skate. A free soul food buffet was on offer. Around 3 AM, the rink cleared out for "roll call," in which skaters showed off different regional styles—JB (James Brown-style skating) from Chicago, fast backwards from Philly/Jersey, Detroit's slide-heavy "open house" variant—while onlookers lined the rails. The event felt convivial, wholesome, about as far from the hedonistic Movement afterparty scene as you could get.

A decade and change later, Soul Skate is on the map as a national skate jam. 2018's edition was basically a small festival, with three rinks and a four-day programme that included things like an indoor picnic, a documentary screening and an adult prom.

"That was truly a mistake," said Kenny Dixon Jr., AKA Moodymann, on Soul Skate's escalation from local party to national festival. I spoke with him in the iconic, purple-curtained house he owns on Grand Boulevard, just across the street from Submerge, a noted local record store and headquarters for Underground Resistance. "Really it started out as, 'How can I put everybody in one room and focus on them buying my T-shirts?'" he said. "I wanna put everybody in there and smother them with my record label, my artists, my T-shirts. That was one of the ideas for Soul Skate, and then that flopped and people didn't give a fuck about my T-shirts or my product or my records. They were like, 'When's your next skate party?'" He laughed. "Yeah, it's its own monster now."

Since the mid-20th century, skating rinks have been an extraordinary staging ground for music and DJ culture, to say nothing of their importance within the civil rights movement and as a gathering space for black communities. As real estate in American cities becomes more scarce and rinks in black neighborhoods disappear, national skate jams like Soul Skate have become a crucial environment for a scene steeped in a tradition that continues to flourish.

Louie Vega, who fell in love with music and DJing as a teenage skater during New York City's early '80s skate boom, returned to the rink to DJ Soul Skate in 2014. "It's beautiful that Moodymann and the Soul Skate team stick to the roots and show where it comes from," he said over the phone. "Skating music has a lot to do with R&B and dance, just as much as discos and house clubs."

Style skating—a skate-dancing style that has splintered into hundreds of regional variants—got its start, in a roundabout way, in Detroit. Bill Butler started skating in 1945 at the Arcadia Ballroom on Woodward Avenue in Detroit on the one night black people were allowed in. At the time, skating rinks were typically scored by chintzy organ music, but on black nights they played records like Count Basie's "Night Train," "Ella Fitzgerald's "Do Nothin' Till You Hear From Me" and Duke Ellington's "C Jam Blues." Years later, as an air force sergeant stationed in Alaska, Butler won money for a pair of skates in a game of craps and started developing his signature "jamma" style, his movements mirroring the solos on the jazz records he'd skate to. He was assigned to an air force station in Brooklyn in 1957 and showed up at the nearest rink, Empire Rollerdrome, where mostly black skaters were rolling to live organ music. He approached the woman in charge and asked if she would play "Night Train." The needle dropped and style skating changed forever.

Legendary skate DJ and Soul Skate regular Big Bob Clayton refers to the now-closed Empire Roller-drome as the "the birthplace of roller disco." Clayton, a New York native, has been DJing for 50 years.

"Most of the dance skating today, you see them holding hands and doing their moves, that's jam skating, that's Bill. That's Bill Butler all day," Clayton said. "I used to go to Empire in '69, but I wasn't worried about DJing in the skate world, I went there because I liked the hustle. I'd go there and dance, I'd skate for the first two hours, then the next two hours, I would hustle in the middle. We were all skaters and dancers, so a friend came to me once in '77 and say, 'Yo Bob, you ever think about DJing in the skate world?' I said, 'Nah man, I'm a club head, I like the club scene.'" He rattled off a list of legendary NYC haunts. "The Loft, Better Days, that's where I liked to be at... I've been playing club music and house music ever since the '70s. That's what I came from."

Clayton started DJing for skaters in '77, eventually landing enviable rink residencies at The Roxy, then at the mecca itself, Empire, both of which were outfitted with soundsystems designed by Richard Long, the legendary audio architect who built the systems at Paradise Garage and Studio 54 in New York and Warehouse in Chicago, to name just a few. Clayton began immersing himself in regional music and skate styles. The folk music anthologist Harry Smith used to have a party trick where he'd identify the county a singer was born in from one verse of a song. Clayton is the skate world equivalent.

"Every state and city had their own style," he said. Locking arms and traversing the rink in trains came from Detroit, for instance. "The hitch-kicking in the line came from Detroit. When you do a bow-legged move like this on your skates"—Clayton spreads his knees in his chair as though he's on skates—"it's called a grapevine. Came out of Detroit. If you want to see all the fast backwards stuff, that came out of South Jersey and Philly, and the Delaware area. I could talk to you about this for hours."

Beginning in the mid-'80s, Clayton traveled to rinks around the US. "I heard about wherever the adults were skating in each city and I would just go. They knew me from Florida to Buffalo, but a lot of cities didn't know who I was when I showed up. I would just pay my money, come in and stand around and I say, 'Oh, they play this here, or they skate like this to that music.' I took notes, I wrote stuff down. Bill gave me the incentive to do that. He traveled all over the country and brought this jamma technique. And that's how I got into the game. So for almost two decades, there was nobody out there but me, because nobody else knew what to do."

As Clayton made strides as a national skate DJ, he remained part of a coterie of NYC DJs and musicians that included Larry Levan, Nicky Siano and Boyd Jarvis. "Even though I was a skate DJ, they knew I loved club and house music, but I made my money in the skate world. Levan was the man. I'd leave Empire at four, five in the morning and go to the Garage. We learned from each other and I brought it to the skate world. When I first started taking out the bass and the highs, all the other DJs around the country at the rinks were like, 'What the hell does he keep doing to the music?'"

Clayton played the adult prom at last year's Soul Skate, holding court in front of a room of skaters who had switched out their wheels for heels and patent leather shoes. He attends every Soul Skate and regularly advises the team of 14 who run the event, which includes Rafael Bryant (Smooth Skatin Ralph), Demarco Bearden (Gadget), Joann Johnson (JoJo), Marcus Gavin (Fresh) and Maurice Dortch (Moe).

"Me and Kenny [Dixon Jr.], we met in the early '90s," Clayton said. "He was skating and hanging out then. This was before he had the record label... Kenny is a beautiful brother. He treats me like a god. He picked me up in a Suburban looking like I'm the president, being whisked through the city. They take good care of me and the respect is there."

The Soul Skate hospitality isn't only afforded to skate legends like Clayton. When I told Dixon Jr. I'd attended various Soul Skate events in 2018, he asked with genuine concern if I'd had a good time and apologized for how hot it had been. "It was way too many people last time," he said. "Apologies for that.

Speaking with Dixon Jr., who has agreed to only two interviews over the last decade, was never a sure thing. We were originally meant to meet up at Detroit Roller Wheels for a morning skate session he frequents, but he was due at DGTL Festival in Amsterdam the next day, and I was informed last-minute he wouldn't be able to make it. Undeterred, I drove out to the rink, a colourful building on an otherwise drab stretch of Schoolcraft St., on a cloudy Friday morning. Inside, a DJ played slow R&B jams like "Get To Know Ya" by Maxwell and "Insanity" by Gregory Porter. Regulars greeted each other with hugs on the side of the rink. A regal older couple glided by with one leg up in perfectly synced figure-skating style.

Traci Washington, Dixon Jr.'s right-hand, turned up a little before noon. After greeting a few skaters, we settled into a booth at the snack bar. I asked her how she got into skating.

"My daughter is now 21, but when she was in middle school, probably 13, they'd have skating trips," she said. "Often times during the day the rinks are reserved for school parties, so I went as a chaper-one. I told Kenny about the party and he came over and once I saw what his body was doing on skates I was like, 'What in the world is going on here? What is that?' He was skating around children, jumping over kids that fell, simultaneously helping kids up, adeptly cutting through crowds of chil-dren. It just made me want to acquire that level—if not that level of skill—just to use my body as a form of art."

She went on: "No matter how tired he is he'll get off a flight from overseas and get to the rink that night. And he'll find skating sessions. If he's in London he'll find a place to skate. So it's a private way for him to enjoy himself. He is extremely humble, he doesn't promote himself or Mahogani Music." She gestured toward the rink. "These people in here don't know anything about Moodymann. They'll just say, 'Hey Kenny, how you doin'?' And he's always happy to see them and they're happy to see him."

At the rink, the swagger of Moodymann's persona slips away. It occurred to me that he's not interest-ed in interviews because he's not interested in self-promotion. He's concerned with giving back to the community, whether it's throwing a BBQ in his backyard or handing out copies of his latest, unre-leased LP. After I left Detroit Roller Wheels, I spoke to him on the phone. We talked about Soul Skate, Big Bob Clayton and that morning's skate session. He told me to come over to his house in an hour. Knocking on the door of his house on Grand, purple curtains blowing in the wind, felt like finally meeting a mythical, Wizard Of Oz-like character.

"That party is for Detroit," Dixon Jr. said. "We take an L every time, it takes us two years to recoup, save up and get money. But we're in the negative every year."

Due to the wave of rink closures, Dixon Jr. explained, skating has become a road trip culture. "For ex-ample, a lot of us skaters travel. But there are a lot of skaters that hear about the out-of-town parties and they can't travel. They don't have the means or the funds. We decided, why don't we just bring it to them? A lot of people ask me, how come you're not DJing or the regular rink DJ is not there? It's because, in a lot of ways, that's the same stuff we hear on a weekly basis. The idea of this here is bringing out-of-town people to Soul Skate is so, one, they can enjoy all the out-of-towners they don't usually get the opportunity to see, and two, so we can show them Detroit hospitality and make sure everyone's having a good time."

At each Soul Skate there's an unannounced headliner at Northland on Saturday night. In 2016, Dixon Jr., dressed immaculately in a white suit and straw campaign hat, introduced hip-hop legend Rakim. In 2018, a curtain dropped, revealing soul music legend Ronald Isley to a screaming, adoring audience gathered on the wood floor of the rink.

I asked Dixon Jr. if the Detroit skaters know he's a house music institution, jetting off to play festivals every weekend. "A few," he said. "It leaks out because you got the internet now. But have I officially come out and agreed to any of that shit? No," he laughed. "Going over there is providing a way for me to do things like this. To give people a concert they didn't even know was coming to them. They might have not seen Rakim. Or, you know, believe it or not, you got people that skate and will skip out on dinner or provide for their children, and I got a full course meal, you know? Try to keep it all night. I got food. Don't leave talkin' about you're hungry, I gotta go and I'm hungry. I got that for you. Don't leave cause you gotta go to a club to see some other thing. I got a concert for you. You ain't gotta go nowhere, it's all tonight baby. Plenty of motherfuckers from all around on the floor."

Back at Detroit Roller Wheels, Washington told me how the national skate community found out about Detroit and Soul Skate. "The largest party in the country was started by a woman from Detroit called Joi," she said. "It's this huge party called Sk8-A-Thon, held during labor day weekend in Atlanta. At these parties, sometimes they'd give the flyers back, they'd say, 'Detroit? No, we're not coming up there.' Because we're known to be aggressive. I mean, we have a very smooth style of skating, but you go to Royal Skateland, these people like to slide, they're very protective of their territory and if you can't skate that style, you might get injured. I would meet hundreds, I would dare say thousands of people who skate and eventually, they got interested in coming here and the word spread."

She continued: "We're one of the few parties that's truly diverse. That's because we're serving house, techno, Moodymann fans and the black skate community throughout the country. Some of the parties around America, they're so big, you can't rent skates, you have to have your own, because they don't want anyone to get injured. We make sure at Soul Skate you can rent skates, because a lot of the people who made this party possible are fans of Moodymann."

Soul Skate is unique in that Dixon Jr., known for producing and DJing club music, is now a recognizable figure within the black skate community. They recognize his afro and sunglasses from Soul Skate T-shirts, not the cover of Silentintroduction. But skating culture is about music as much as it's about style skating and community.

"A good skate DJ plays like your parents at home,'" Dixon Jr. said. "They play like back in the '70s when you went to a club and they played everything. See, I can go to a club, get down, sweat, 'Boy, that shit was exciting,' me and my friends we would get down. We would have a great time, talk to the ladies… At the skate rink, they gonna slow it down, they gonna break it down, they gonna break it all the way down. You ain't gonna hear no slow jams at the club no more. Back in the '70s and '80s they'd rock you for about two hours and they'll break it back down."

Dixon Jr.'s sprawling Prince collection was neatly displayed on the walls around us at his Grand Blvd. house. "You're telling me you're not gonna play no 'Do Me Baby' in this bitch? The fuck? Fuck that."

The style of DJing Dixon Jr. is referring to has its roots in New York City's post-disco scene, when the loose, slowed-down sound developing on singles from classic Big Apple labels like Prelude worked just as well, or better, at the rink as they did in the club. The development of skate music from the late '70s up to the present is intertwined with the roots of dance music, as nuanced and colourful as any sub-genre.

FEEL GOOD MUSIC

Happy Songs To Boost Your Mood

Need a pick-me-up? These songs guaranteed to lift your mood. You'll like them even if you're already feeling good, too!

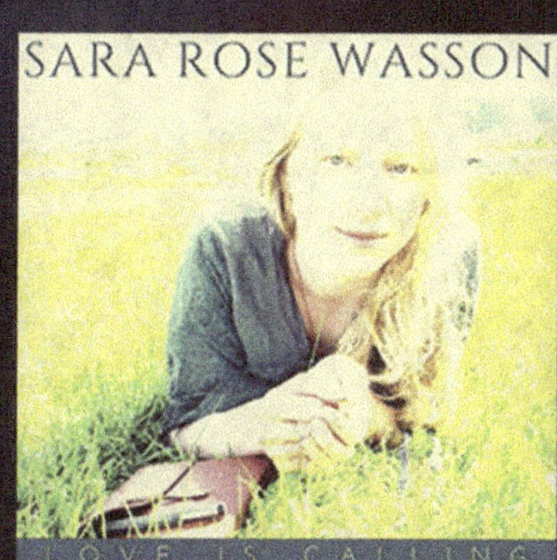

ANEESSA
GONNA BE ALRIGHT

SARA ROSE WASSON
LOVE IS CALLING

MITCHELL COLEMAN JR.
GET FUNKY

WWW.PUMPITUPMAGAZINE.COM/RADIO

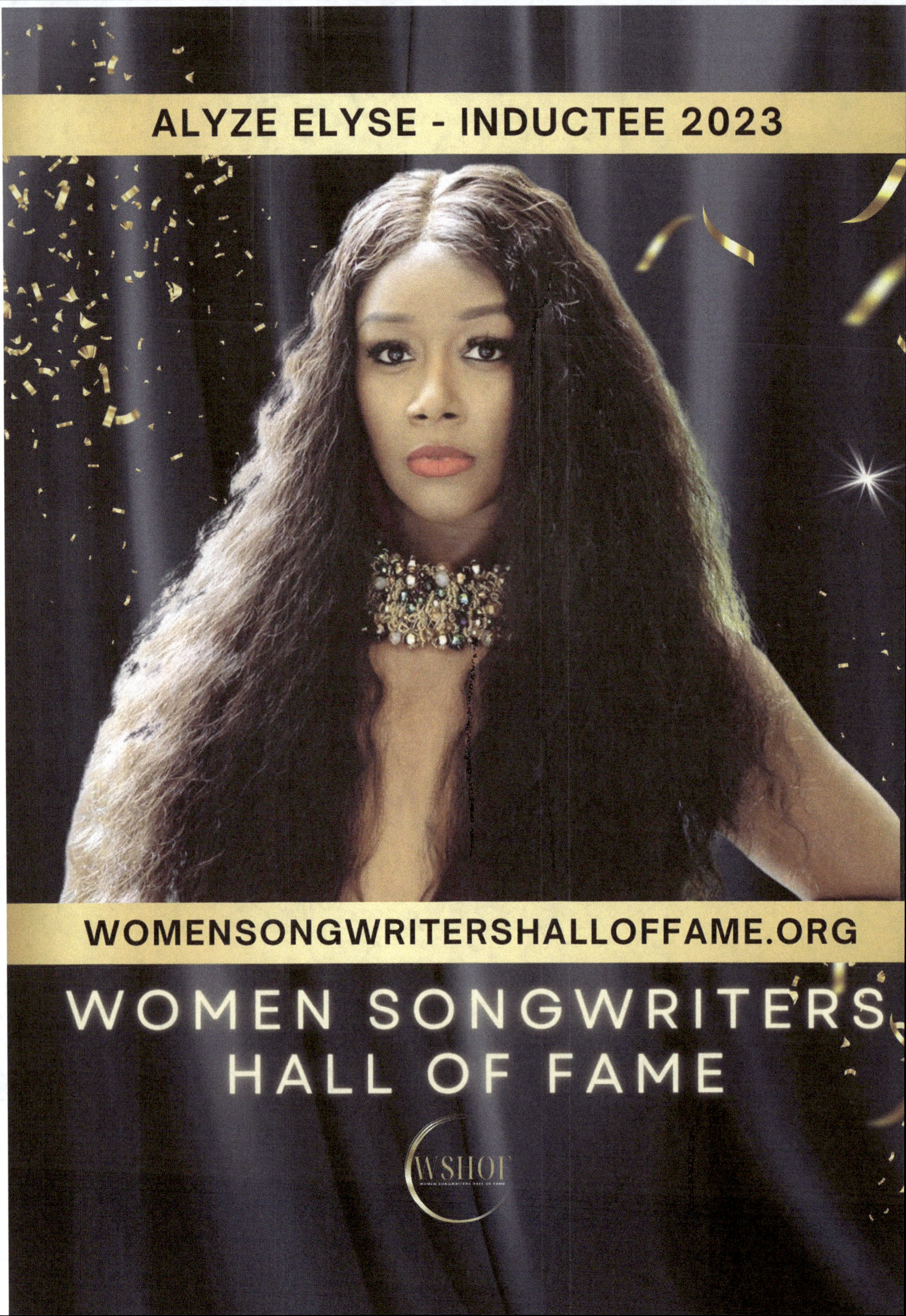

ALYZE ELYSE - INDUCTEE 2023
WOMENSONGWRITERSHALLOFFAME.ORG
WOMEN SONGWRITERS
HALL OF FAME

TOP

TOP INDIE ARTISTS

R&B - POP - SOUL - BLUES MUSIC

ANEESSA
"Gonna be Alright"
Better Days Mix

SARA ROSE WASSON
"Love is Calling"

H'ATINA
"Journey"

MINISTER PHYLLIS MCMEANS
"Help"

JOCELYN AKER
"Never Ready"

MICHAEL B. SUTTON
"Feelin Down"

TUNE IN ON
PUMP IT UP MAGAZINE RADIO

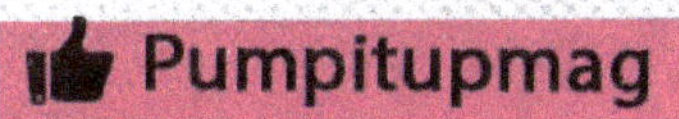
Pumpitupmag

Pumpitupmagazine

Pumpitupmagazine.

WWW.PUMPITUPMAGAZINE.COM

DELIT FACE

Social Media For The Entertainment World

MUSIC & MOVIE Industry

SINGER
SONGWRITER
MUSICIANS
PRODUCERS
PUBLISHERS
DISTRIBUTORS
MUSIC SUPERVISORS

ACTORS
DIRECTORS
PRODUCERS
DISTRIBUTORS
SET DESIGNERS
SCRIPT
WRITERS
EXTRAS

MAKE UP ARTISTS
HAIR STYLISTS
PHOTOGRAPHERS
GRAPHIC DESIGNER

Register now FREE and connect with people in your industry
www.delitface.com

Bilingual Book Store

FRENCH - ENGLISH

www.bilingualbookstore.com

"Dust off your
bell bottoms
&
Let's party like
it's 1976!"
Aneessa

Spotify amazon iTunes
TIDAL

Gonna
Be
Alright
ANEESSA

Funky	Trendy	Cool	Hip

Wear The Music You Love!

Visit our merchandise store on our website:

WWW.FUNKTHERAPYMUSIC.COM

10% Discount code: STAYFUNKY

- Hoodies
- Crop Top
- Sweat Pants
- Bucket Hats
- Slides
- Mugs

UNISEX T–SHIRTS

Brown T–Shirt

Orange T–Shirt

Beige T–Shirts

Join our community
@funktherapy2

HOW TO LOOK EXPENSIVE ON A BUDGET

1. WEAR BLACK

Black is a neutral, it goes with everything. Since it is a solid color it coordinates with other colors and patterns. When we think of the color black, we think of Coco Chanel. She made the colors black and white famous in her tailored clothes and fabrics.

2. MONOCHROME IT OUT

One of the easiest ways to add extra spice to an outfit is with tonal or monochrome pieces. Theodora often styles her clients in identical colored tops and skirts while changing the textures to add a bit of dimension. Monochrome outfits are not only incredibly elongating, but they look effortless, put together, and very expensive.

3. ADD A BLAZER

Amanda Greyson, style director at Free People, believes blazers are the surefire way at elevating even the simplest of outfits. "Try adding a blazer to a simple hoodie and denim look, finishing with a baseball hat and high-top trainers," she suggests. "This will instantly make your look feel more luxe for all those weekend errands. Or, for date night, add an oversized blazer to a silk black dress and easy bootie."

4. WEAR PIECES THAT FIT WELL

Always make sure your clothes fit well. If you have an hourglass figure, wear pieces that fit showing off your curves. If you have a few pounds in areas you want to conceal, opt for pieces that are slightly loose and flow when you walk. For all figures, avoid wearing clothes that are too loose..

5. SPLURGE ON A STRONG BLACK COAT

Invest in classic, high-quality outerwear in timeless black or camel colorways. It will last you decades. Classic styles never expire and will carry you through every decade—warm.

6. WEAR POINTED FLATS OR HEELS

Women who wear flats or heels that are pointed have a look that screams expensive! Black or nude are popular colors that go with everything. They are considered wardrobe essentials.

6. WEAR LIPCOLOR

Wear makeup that looks natural and wear lipcolor. Wear a lipcolor that has a colored tint, like red, coral or pink. Red is a classic lipcolor. It goes great with black and white. Wear a shade of red that looks good with your skin tone. Make sure your nails are kept trimmed and/or painted.

7. COORDINATE YOUR SHOES & BAG

A key to making your outfits look polished is coordinating your shoes and bag. If you wear black shoes then carry a black bag. Brown shoes look great with a brown bag in the same color tone. You can venture out a bit by wearing black shoes with a nude or a solid color bag, like pink. Leopard flats or heels look great with a black or nude bag.

8. WEAR SUNGLASSES

Wear sunglasses and you'll look cool and collected! Perhaps the images of celebrities wearing beautiful sunglasses have been an influence to us to wear them.
The fancier the sunglasses help make your outfit look expensive. black sunglasses, aviator sunglasses, cat-eye sunglasses, leopard sunglasses

9. WEAR STATEMENT JEWELRY

Wear jewelry that makes a statement.
Fancy jewelry adds a polished look to any outfit. When your outfit is basic, like black pants and a white top, add a statement necklace, earrings bracelet and you outfit instantly looks "glam"!

FITNESS
25 - 34
GET IN SHAPE
FUN WAYS TO
TO EXERCISE THIS SUMMER
Pump it up Magazine / 25 - 34

EXERCISE IN SUMMER THAT WON'T FEEL LIKE A CHORE!

ROLLERSKATING

Roller skating is an aerobic workout that increases coordination and balance. This retro pastime doesn't just look cool, it also leaves your body feeling great.

1

BIKE RIDE

Whether you're one of our crazy intense cyclers in our PK fam, or just down for a slower family ride along the beach- biking is an excellent workout, and so much fun!

2

FAVORITE CHILDHOOD GAME

Nothing like taking yourself back to days when the living was easy! There is a part of me that will never give up on capture the flag no matter how old. I just wish someone would ask me to play (hint, hint).

3

DANCING (ZUMBA, SWING..)

Ready to try something new? Join a dance class! When you leave I promise you'll be weating up a storm, and the best part is dancing is so fun!

4

HAVE A WALKING MEETING

Do you often plan meetings with your coworkers to just sit around and talk? Take that meeting outside and talk as you go for a group walk!

5

HIKING

There is nothing like a good hike, the burn in your legs, the fresh air, the views. Hiking will never feel like a chore to me, more of a release from everyday life!

6

ACTIVE VIDEO GAMES

Active video games are truly the best! They're so fun, and you can really work up a sweat quick if you do it right!

7

HAVE FUN!

WHAT IS MICRONEEDLING FACIAL?

EVERYTHING YOU NEED TO KNOW

Microneedling. The minimally invasive treatment can be used all over the body—from scalp to ankles—to improve the appearance of scars, boost collagen, or encourage hair growth. Microneedling creates microscopic punctures in the skin.

MICRONEEDLING STIMULATES DORMANT HAIR FOLLICLES.

The stimulation of dormant hair follicles equals new hair growth, confirms Gohara. In a recent study, 100 test subjects were divided into two groups. One set was treated with minoxidil lotion, and the other received minoxidil lotion plus microneedling. After 12 weeks, 82 percent of the microneedling group reported a 50 percent improvement versus 4.5 percent of the minoxidil lotion-only group.

MICRONEEDLING CAN ALSO WORK TO REDUCE CELLULITE.

Alexiades works with a new crop of microneedling devices like the Profound by Candela. She uses the machine for crepe-like fine lines as well as sagging skin and cellulite.

YOUR DERMAROLLER PLAYS WELL WITH OTHER SKINCARE TREATMENTS.

Alexiades recommends pairing microneedling with topical treatments (like her 37 Extreme Actives anti-aging cream or serum) and lasers. "Often, we use this as an opportunity to apply anti-aging preparations that will penetrate better through the needle punctures. When you combine with topicals, you have a shot at some collagen building. When combined with radiofrequency, you can see tissue tightening over months," she says.

YOU NEED TO BE GENTLE ON YOUR SKIN AFTER MICRONEEDLING.

"Let the skin chill after microneedling," Gohara says. "For the rest of the day, don't wash the skin, expose it to high heat, sweat too much (that means no sun, no gym, no hot yoga)."

MICRONEEDLING ALONE ONLY GIVES TEMPORARY RESULTS.

Dr. Alexiades notes that a recent AAD study showed that microneeedling alone can only give temporary results that do not last. "As my over ten years of research has shown, you must combine microneedles with radiofrequency to get long term wrinkle and scar reductions and improvements in skin quality," explains Alexiades.

WEST END ORGANIX

Ageless Beauty, Organic Health

BLACK SEED OIL

HEALTHY IMMUNE SYSTEM
INFLAMMATORY RESPONSE

www.westendorganix.com

Photo by cottonbro studio

In the 1960s, Thomas, a young musician/producer, fell in love with Emily, a charismatic singer, despite her past struggles. They got married and had three children, appearing to be a perfect family. However, behind closed doors, Emily became an abusive and controlling partner, causing Thomas deep emotional wounds and leading to his mental health deterioration.

Thomas sought therapy to find relief, but the true cause of his afflictions remained hidden until he underwent hypnosis. He discovered that Emily was the source of his agoraphobia and panic attacks, resulting from years of manipulation and abuse. This revelation both shook him and empowered him to recognize the toxic nature of their relationship.

Thomas had severe agoraphobia, isolating himself from the outside world and missing out on connections and experiences. In 1999, he initiated divorce proceedings to break free from Emily's control. However, she continued to exert influence, refusing to let go of his name and interfering in his life.

In 2017, Thomas met Marie, the love of his life, and they got married. Marie became his pillar of support, helping him on his healing journey. Together, they explored various therapies and techniques, gradually unraveling the trauma inflicted by Emily's abuse.

Thomas's healing journey faced obstacles due to Emily's attempts to sabotage his happiness. But he and Marie set firm boundaries, sought therapy, and fortified their bond. They emerged as a testament to resilience and perseverance.

Emily's abuse also affected Thomas's relationship with his children, except for his daughter Nathaly, who defied her mother's control and fought for a connection with him. Nathaly's bravery inspired Thomas to confront the truth and break free from the cycle of abuse.

Thomas and Marie channeled their love for music into a thriving career, establishing their own music label. They traveled the world, performed their music, and shared their story of triumph.

Thomas's story is a testament to resilience, as he overcame narcissistic abuse, agoraphobia, and reclaimed his passion for music with the support of Marie and Nathaly. His journey aims to inspire others facing similar challenges to pursue healing, self-discovery, and the pursuit of passion.

Read the story in full detail on our wellness section at pumpitupmagazine.com/wellness.

Tips For Taking Care Of Your
MENTAL HEALTH
C-PTSD & NARCISSISTIC ABUSE

People who have Narcissistic Personality Disorder have damaged self-esteem that is easily harmed by even small criticisms.
They are continually looking to shore up their weak areas of self-opinion.
To accomplish this need for self-preservation, they abuse and use other people, including, unfortunately, their own children, significant others etc..

Recognize the trait of the narcissist

A sense of uniqueness
Boastful behavior
Exaggeration of their talents
Grandiose fantasies
A sense of superiority
Self-centered behavior
Self-referential behavior
A deep need for attention and admiration

Recognize the trait of The covert narcissist

Passive Self-Importance
Blaming and Shaming
Creating Confusion
Procrastination and Disregard
(The covert narcissist is a professional
at not acknowledging you at all.)
Giving With a Goal (to make themselves look good)
Emotionally Neglectful

How to Deal With a Narcissist

Set Boundaries
Avoid Taking It Personally
Advocate for Yourself
Create a Healthy Distance
Seek Help – Talk to a Therapist
Remove the Heart Wall
Emotion Codean energy healing technique
for releasing trapped emotion

C-PTSD
Complex Post Traumatic Stress Disorder

is more severe if:
the traumatic events happened early in life
the trauma was caused by a wife/husband/parent
the person experienced the trauma for a long time
the person was alone during the trauma
there's still contact with the person
responsible for the trauma

Symptoms of complex PTSD

Anxiety – Agoraphobia – Panic Attack
Alcoholism–Drug Abuse
Negative thoughts about
yourself, other people or the world
Hopelessness about the future
Memory problems,
Difficulty maintaining close relationships
Feeling detached from family and friends
Lack of interest in activities you once enjoyed
Difficulty experiencing positive emotions
Feeling emotionally numb

How to Treat complex PTSD

Set Boundaries
Avoid Taking It Personally
Advocate for Yourself
Create a Healthy Distance
Seek Help – Talk to a Therapist
Remove the Heart Wall
with the help of a Healer

@pumpitupmagazine
www.pumpitupmagazine.com

MY MUSIC LIST

____
A SONG THAT MAKES ME HAPPY

____
A SONG FROM THE 70s

____
A SONG ABOUT YOUR COUNTRY

____
A SONG WITH A COLOR

____
A SONG YOU CAN'T LISTEN ANYMORE

SHARE THIS LIST WITH YOUR FRIENDS

ALBUM CHALLENGE

____
DEBUT ALBUM

____
CONCEPT ALBUM

____
80'S ALBUM

____
LIVE ALBUM

____
SOUNDTRACK

____
FAVORITE ALBUM

This or That

What would you choose?

Get up early or Stay up late

Talk to dogs or Talk to cats

Lose your sense of taste or Lose your sense of smell

Give up on music or Give up on movies

Read minds or Know everything

Travel to the future or Travel to the past

WHAT WOULD YOU PREFER...
RANDOM EDITION

Live in the city or Live in the countryside

Play video games or Play board games

Lose your phone or Lose your wallet

Speak many languages or Speak with animals

Own a private island or Own a private jet

Live without music or Live without TV

EATING WELL FOR MENTAL HEALTH

You've probably heard the phrase "Food is Medicine". This famous phrase comes from Ancient Greek physician Hippocrates, "Let food be thy medicine, and let medicine be thy food" and with so many processed and unhealthy options available, it's never been more important.

We all know proper nutrition is good for our bodies. We know it helps us build muscle, stay fit, maintain healthy skin, and keep our energy stable. But somehow we always treat our minds as if they're separate from our bodies, and our mental health separate from the food we eat.

But more and more, we're discovering the direct relationship between our nutrition and our anxiety, depression, clarity, and happiness. It's even developing into its own field Nutritional Psychology. Why? Because our brains are the center of everything.

Think about it. Your brain is always "on." It takes care of your thoughts and movements, your breathing and heartbeat, your senses — it works hard 24/7, even while you're asleep. This means your brain requires a constant supply of fuel. That "fuel" comes from the foods you eat — and what's in that fuel makes all the difference. Put simply, what you eat directly affects the structure and function of your brain and, ultimately, your mood.

What do you eat for Mental Health?

First of all, know that you can't be perfect every day. Sometimes being a little imperfect and enjoying some foods or drinks that are "not ideal for your mental health" is part of living a healthy balanced life.

At MacroPlate.com, we often emphasize the 80/20 rule. Make sure your healthy life choices fill 80% of your lifestyle, and your "live-a-little" choices satisfy that other 20%.

But in general, a diet full of rich plant-based foods with grains, fruits, and veggies, combined with healthy protein sources, and plenty of good clean fats is the best way to go.

However, some foods stand above and beyond others as being nutritionally dense with micronutrients that really benefit and support a healthy mind and mood.

The Best Foods for Mental Health

Oatmeal

While your body and brain utilize carbohydrates for energy, too often we consume simple carbs, which lead to blood sugar spikes. Foods classified as whole grains contain complex carbohydrates, which leads to glucose being produced more slowly, as a more even and consistent source of energy.

Also, oats help the brain absorb tryptophan, which helps reduce the symptoms of depression and anxiety while boosting brain function.

Salmon

Fish, in general, is a healthy choice, but salmon is at the top of the list. It's a "fatty" fish, containing high amounts of omega-3 fatty acids, which have been linked to a reduction in mental disorders such as depression. Omega-3s have been shown to boost learning and memory as well.

EATING WELL FOR MENTAL HEALTH

Brocoli Sprouts

Broccoli Sprouts are nature's miracle food. So much so, we've already written a whole blog about them. They're actually one of the healthiest plant compounds on earth, with off-the-chart concentrated levels nutrients that have been proven to provide many nutritional benefits from brain-boosting anti-aging, preventing memory loss, treating depression, and improving the brain function of autism.

Walnuts

When eaten in moderation, most nuts are a good source of heart-healthy monounsaturated fats as well as protein. But walnuts get the edge when it comes to lessening the symptoms of depression because they also are one of the richest plant-based sources of omega-3 fatty acids. "The omega-3s in walnuts support overall brain health," says Robin H-C.

Yogurt

Probiotics are beneficial bacteria that exist naturally in foods like yogurt and kimchi. While we're familiar with how they impact our gut health, there's new evidence that they're also really beneficial for our mental health. Studies suggest that probiotics, as found in yogurt, may reduce the risk of depression by boosting the production of serotonin from an amino acid, tryptophan.

Berries

Berries, specifically blueberries and blackberries are full of antioxidants which are outstanding at mitigating depression. And luckily, the effects are immediate. In recent studies, blueberries improved positive affect – a measure of positive moods such as joy, interest, and alertness – 2-hours after consumption.

Banana

Eating potassium-rich foods such, as pumpkin seeds or bananas, may help reduce symptoms of stress and anxiety. They also help with mood balance and depression. The two key components in bananas are vitamin B-6 and tryptophan. Separately, they work to reduce depressive symptoms, and together, they form a dynamic duo of brain chemistry to send you tons of positive vibes.

Chocolate

No, it's not just because chocolate makes us feel good. Dark chocolate can help reduce anxiety and improve symptoms of clinical depression. People who ate dark chocolate in two 24-hour periods had 70% reduced odds of reporting depressive symptoms than those who did not eat chocolate. Remember that the cacao is the important bit, so avoid really milky chocolates that are mostly cream and sugar.

Apricots

Apricots are rich in magnesium, which acts a natural stress-buster and helps to calm tensed muscles. A deficiency of magnesium is known to cause headaches and leaves you fatigued. Apricots contain Vitamin B that helps to cure nervous system disorders like hyperactivity, memory loss and mental fatigue.

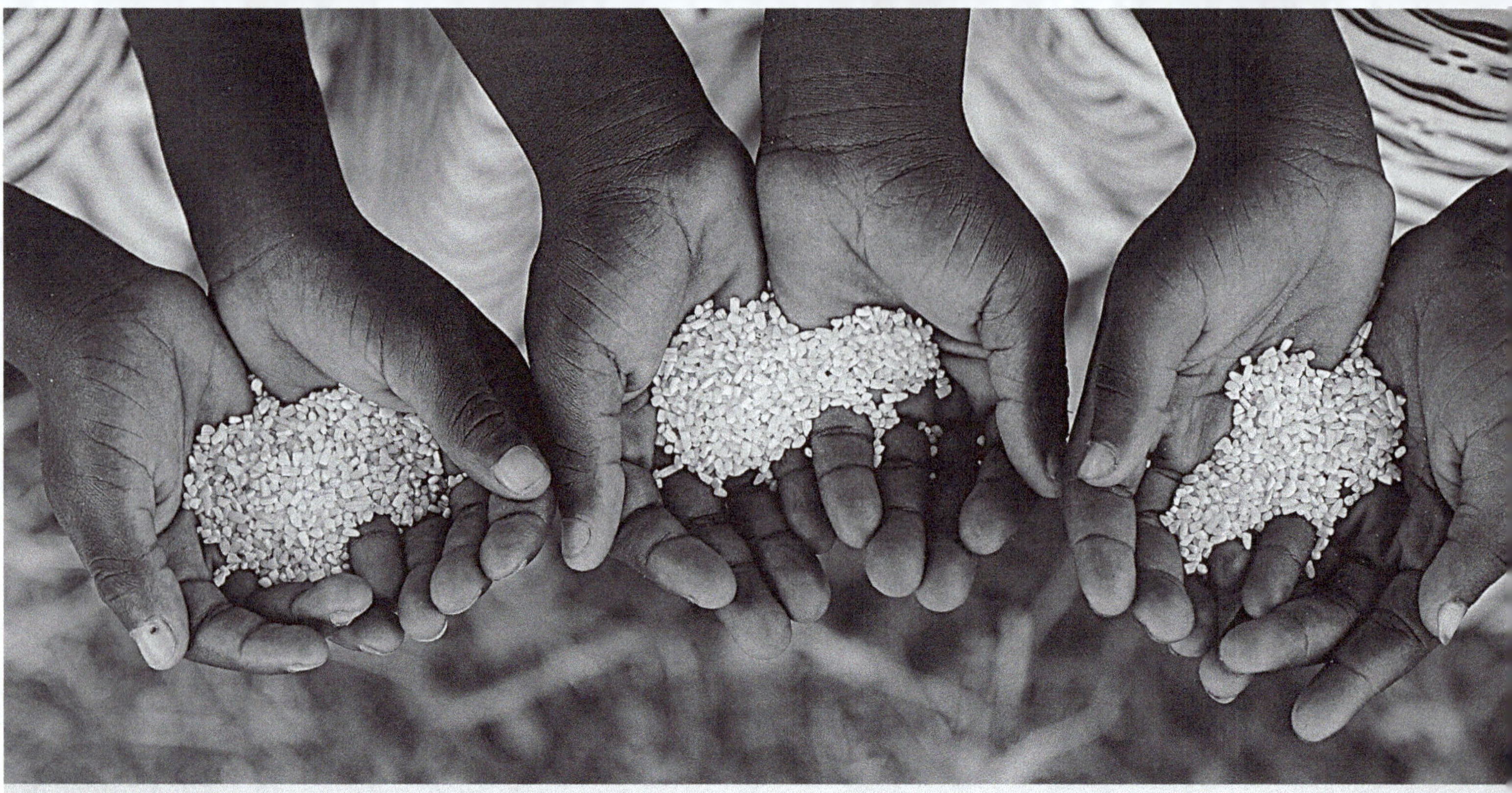

HELP STOP HUNGER & POVERTY

There are 1 billion impoverished kids around the world

JOIN OUR CAMPAIGN TO HELP GIVE THEM BETTER LIVES.